School Days
Then and Now

Bobbie Kalman

Crabtree Publishing Company

www.crabtreebooks.com

Created by Bobbie Kalman

Dedicated by Samantha Crabtree
For Kiera Wilson
I hope you like your new school in Alberta.
I love you and miss you a lot.

Author and Editor-in-Chief
Bobbie Kalman

Editors
Kathy Middleton
Crystal Sikkens

Photo research
Bobbie Kalman

Design
Bobbie Kalman
Samantha Crabtree
Katherine Berti
Samara Parent (front cover)

Prepress technician
Katherine Berti

Print coordinator
Margaret Amy Salter

Illustrations and reproductions
Barbara Bedell: back cover (bottom), pages 1, 17 (top right), 19 (top right), 21 (bottom), 22
Antoinette "Cookie" Bortolon: page 15
Detail from Country Schoolhouse, 1879, ©Morgan Weistling, licensed by The Greenwich Workshop, Inc. www.greenwichworkshop.com: pages 4–5
Bonna Rouse: page 19 (bottom right)

Photographs
Digital Stock: page 6 (top left)
Image Club Graphics: page 19 (bottom left)
Library of Congress: LC-DIG-nclc-04337: page 9 (left)
Thinkstock: back cover (top), pages 1 (top left and right), 13 (top left)
Wikimedia Commons: Beurret & Bailly: page 15 (top right inset); Terra Foundation for American Art: page 21 (top)
Front cover and all other images by Shutterstock

Library and Archives Canada Cataloguing in Publication

Kalman, Bobbie, author
     School days then and now / Bobbie Kalman.

(From olden days to modern ways in your community)
Includes index.
Issued in print and electronic formats.
ISBN 978-0-7787-0127-9 (bound).--ISBN 978-0-7787-0209-2 (pbk.).
--ISBN 978-1-4271-9416-9 (pdf).--ISBN 978-1-4271-9410-7 (html)

     1. Schools--Juvenile literature. I. Title.

LB1556.K345 2013   j372   C2013-906096-0
                                        C2013-906097-9

Library of Congress Cataloging-in-Publication Data

Kalman, Bobbie.
 School days then and now / Bobbie Kalman.
     pages cm. -- (From olden days to modern ways in your community)
 Includes index.
 ISBN 978-0-7787-0127-9 (reinforced library binding) -- ISBN 978-0-7787-0209-2 (pbk.) -- ISBN 978-1-4271-9416-9 (electronic pdf) -- ISBN 978-1-4271-9410-7 (electronic html)
 1. Schools--History--Juvenile literature. I. Title.

 LA11.K25 2013
 371.009--dc23
                                        2013034935

Crabtree Publishing Company
www.crabtreebooks.com   1-800-387-7650

Printed in Canada/042018/MQ20180319

Copyright © **2014 CRABTREE PUBLISHING COMPANY**. All rights reserved. No part of this publication may be reproduced, stored in a retrieval system or be transmitted in any form or by any means, electronic, mechanical, photocopying, recording, or otherwise, without the prior written permission of Crabtree Publishing Company. In Canada: We acknowledge the financial support of the Government of Canada through the Canada Book Fund for our publishing activities.

Published in Canada
Crabtree Publishing
616 Welland Ave.
St. Catharines, Ontario
L2M 5V6

Published in the United States
Crabtree Publishing
PMB 59051
350 Fifth Avenue, 59th Floor
New York, New York 10118

Published in the United Kingdom
Crabtree Publishing
Maritime House
Basin Road North, Hove
BN41 1WR

Published in Australia
Crabtree Publishing
3 Charles Street
Coburg North
VIC 3058

What is in this book?

4

Old and new schools

Long ago, there were huge areas of the country where very few people lived. Most people in these places were farmers. One of the first buildings that people in a new **community** built was a school for their children.

Communities today need schools, too. The schools are different from schools long ago, but, in some ways, they are the same. How is this classroom the same as yours? What things do you see that are different?

One room or many?

A one-room school was small. Students helped keep it clean.

This schoolhouse from long ago had only one room and one teacher. Children of all ages learned together. Electricity had not yet been invented, so a stove heated the school in winter. Open windows kept it cool on warm days.

Sometimes, an entire school had only a few students.

School rooms today

Not many schools today have just one room. Most have several classrooms. Besides classrooms, schools also have libraries, **gymnasiums**, offices, washrooms, and lunchrooms. There are also special rooms for teachers.

This large school has many rooms.

How many rooms?

Make a list of the rooms in your school. Where do you spend most of your time? Which is your favorite room at school?

Classrooms today often have many students. How many are in your class?

7

Getting to school

Students today walk, ride bicycles, or get rides to school from their parents or other adults. Many children take a school bus each day. They enjoy talking to their friends on the way to school.

This girl rides her bike to school. She wears a helmet to be safe.

Would you fly to school if you could?

A very long walk!

Long ago, there were no cars, school buses, or even bicycles for getting children to school! Most children had to walk more than an hour to reach their school from their home. In winter, snowstorms made it hard for them to see where they were going. Children often arrived at school with very cold toes!

These children had more than a two-hour walk to their school. They are carrying their lunches in tin pails.

How far?

How far is your school from your home? How do you take your lunch to school? Do you use a lunch box?

9

School helpers

In a school today, there are several teachers, as well as a librarian, school nurse, principal, and caretaker. Bus drivers and crossing guards also work for schools.

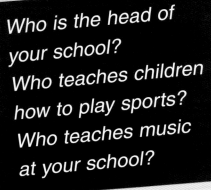

Who teaches physical education?

Who is the head of your school?
Who teaches children how to play sports?
Who teaches music at your school?

Who takes care of you when you are sick at school?

Just one teacher

In one-room schools, there was just one teacher who taught all the children. There was no principal or librarian. Parents paid the teacher's **salary**, or pay, and families took turns giving the teacher a place to live in their homes.

What would you miss?

If you went to a one-room school, what things would you miss that you have at your school now?

A teacher taught up to eight grades in one class and also had to keep the school clean. The students and some parents helped out.

11

A school day

Science is a subject that children learn today.

Students today come to school in the morning, have recess, and take a lunch break. Besides reading, writing, and math, they also learn science, art, social studies, music, and physical education. Children do their schoolwork with the help of books and computers.

Make a calendar of your school activities for one week. Then create a list of your favorite activities.

Time to start school!

In a one-room school long ago, the teacher rang a school bell to let the children know that school was about to begin.

Children practiced their lessons by reciting what the teacher taught them.

Very few subjects

Students learned reading, writing, spelling, and **arithmetic**, or math, and some social studies and science. Children learned by copying what the teacher wrote on the blackboard and **reciting**, or repeating out loud, what they were taught. Schools had very few books because books were expensive, and farmers did not have much money. Often, each child had one book called a **primer**.

This girl is using a primer.

13

Learning tools

Many schools today have laptop computers, tablets, printers, and **interactive whiteboards** to help children read, write, spell, and learn different subjects. They can also create their reports on them.

Children long ago wrote on slates, or small blackboards (see opposite page). Digital tablets are the same shape, but how are they different?

This boy is using a special pen to write his answers on an interactive whiteboard, which is connected to his teacher's laptop.

This girl has found information and pictures about one-room schools on her laptop.

Write and wipe

In one-room schools, students wrote their lessons on slates, using slate pencils or chalk. After each lesson, they wiped their slates clean, so they could use them again. They could not keep their work and look at it again. How did this make learning harder?

slate and slate pencil

On their slates, children copied the letters and words the teacher wrote.

15

Fun ways to learn

Today, there are many fun ways to learn. Children draw, paint, write stories, and play musical instruments. Students from different **cultures** share their ways of life through stories, music, and art. Students also play learning games at school on computers or digital tablets.

This girl is playing a math game on her tablet.

*These students drew a map of the world to show the countries and **continents** where they were born. They enjoyed learning about the world and about one another.*

Word games

Spelling was an important subject long ago, just as it is today. It helped children become better readers and writers. **Spelling bees** were popular in the past and are still popular now. Children also played word games, such as Anagrams. Anagrams helped them become better spellers.

In the game of Anagrams, children switch letters around to make different words, such as tale and late, pest and step.

In a spelling bee, children in a class take turns spelling words given to them by the teacher. They stand until they make a mistake, and then they have to sit down. Only two students are left in this spelling bee.

Games and sports

Games and sports are a big part of school today because exercise keeps students healthy. At recess, children play clapping and skipping games. After school, they play baseball, basketball, and soccer.

Did you know?

Basketball was invented in 1891 by James Naismith, a Canadian sports coach. The first basketball nets were peach baskets.

Clapping games are fun to play.

Still played today

Many games and sports that were played at school in the past are still played now. The boys on the right are playing baseball. The girls below right are playing a clapping game. Other favorite recess games were tag, leapfrog, tug of war, and many kinds of skipping games.

What safety equipment would these boys be wearing if they were playing baseball today?

skipping

leapfrog

Clapping games have been played for hundreds of years.

Gardens of health

These students grew nutritious vegetables such as lettuce, tomatoes, peppers, cucumbers, and onions in their school garden. Learning to cook healthy recipes is the next step.

Most schools today teach children about **nutrition**. Growing vegetable gardens is an important part of this subject. Does your school have a garden? School gardens teach students:

- about nature
- how plants make food
- how to work as a team
- how to measure spaces between plants so the plants have room to grow

Which foods does your body need to stay healthy? Which foods should you eat less often?

Farming lessons at school

Many people long ago were farmers, and their children would also become farmers. Growing vegetable gardens at school gave children farming skills and also provided them with food. Students used the vegetables to make meals at school. They stored some to make hot soups in winter.

The students at this school are growing carrots, onions, pumpkins, potatoes, and sunflowers. How is this school yard different from your school yard?

Last day of school

Children long ago celebrated the end of the school year. They learned special songs, put on plays, and played games with family and friends. Today, students celebrate the end of the school year in similar ways. Some have a party with their friends and look forward to coming back the following school year. Others **graduate** from elementary school and go on to high school. What do you like to do on the last day of school?

This child graduated from kindergarten.

These families are celebrating the last day of school long ago with races, fun games, and a picnic of delicious foods that everyone enjoyed.

Learn more

Books

Kalman, Bobbie. *My Community Long Ago* (My World). Crabtree Publishing, 2011

Kalman, Bobbie. *My School Community* (My World). Crabtree Publishing, 2010.

Kalman, Bobbie and Heather Levigne. *Schoolyard Games* (Historic Communities) Crabtree Publishing, 2001.

Kalman, Bobbie and Heather Levigne. *Classroom Games* (Historic Communities). Crabtree Publishing, 2001.

Kalman, Bobbie. *School from A to Z* (AlphaBasiCs). Crabtree Publishing, 1999.

Kalman, Bobbie. *A One-Room School* (Historic Communities). Crabtree Publishing, 1994.

Websites

Read a letter from a student in 1901 describing what her school was like and what she thought school would be like 100 years from then at: www.dltk-kids.com/pioneer/school_in_the_1800.htm

Learn more about one-room schools long ago at: *www.aitc.sk.ca/saskschools/school.html*

Find out more about one-room schools, including information on teachers then and now, yard games, and personal stories from students at: *www.oneroomschoolhouses.ca/index.html*

Words to know

Note: Some boldfaced words are defined where they appear in the book.

arithmetic Mathematics, such as addition, subtraction, multiplication, and division

community A group of people who live together in one area and share buildings, services, and a way of life; The place in which these people live

continent One of the seven huge areas of land on Earth

culture The customs, beliefs, and the way of life of a group of people

gymnasium A room with equipment for indoor sports or exercise

primer A first textbook for teaching reading or arithmetic

recite To repeat aloud from memory

salary Money paid to a person on a regular basis for doing a job

interactive whiteboard A large board connected to a computer on which people control the computer by using their fingers or a special pen

spelling bee A game or competition in which players must spell words correctly to continue

nutrition Healthy food that gives the body energy and helps it grow

graduate To finish a stage of education

Index